The

MIRACLES

EBED
PUBLICATIONS
In love, serve one another

by

ANNIE HILL DAVIS

EBED Publications is a ministry of The McDougal
Foundation, Inc., a Maryland nonprofit corporation
dedicated to spreading the Gospel of the Lord Jesus
Christ to as many people as possible in the shortest
time possible.

Published by:

EBED Publications
P.O. Box 3595
Hagerstown, MD 21742-3595

ISBN 1-884369-83-9

Printed in the United States of America
For Worldwide Distribution

DEDICATION

I would like to dedicate this book to my beloved husband of thirty-seven years, John William Davis. I thank God for him.

To all the children with whom God has blessed me: Gerald, Jimmy, Sue, Bobby, and Brenda Carol Davis.

To my son-in-law, Matthew, and my daughters-in-law, Sheila, Lora, and Brenda Kay Davis.

To all my grandchildren, especially Joshua, whom God healed of spinal meningitis when he was only three months old.

To my sisters, Fannie Davis and Mildred Walters, who have supported me and encouraged me with their prayers and finances.

To my brothers, W. H. and Herman Hill.

To everyone else who has helped through their prayers, finances, encouragement or in any other way.

A special thanks to my daughter, Brenda Carol, who was kept awake while I sat up late many nights typing. She also helped to finance this project, encouraged me with her prayers, did some of the typing and proof-read my stories.

Most of all, I thank the Lord, without whose help, this work would not have been possible. May all the glory be unto Him.

CONTENTS

INTRODUCTION

One day when I accompanied my son to the hospital emergency room after an accident to see if he might have injured his hand, I struck up a conversation with a stranger, a lady whose parents had been Christians. She was very interested in hearing what God had done for me and my family. As I told her the miracles I could remember (there are many that I have forgotten), she was blessed in the hearing of them, and I was blessed in the retelling of them.

I had already written down some simple stories of miracles, and I had that writing in my purse. When I pulled it out and let her read it, she enjoyed it and was blessed by it. I became convinced that day that others would be blessed as well by the retelling of some of the miracles God has done for us, and I decided to show my gratitude to the Lord for His great blessings by telling them to others.

We are just very simple people with simple language and simple life-styles, but God has proven to us over and over again that He loves simple people and is interested in our lives, down to the smallest details.

Some of these stories may seem too simple for some, or even unimportant, but believe me, nothing about our lives is unimportant to God. He is willing to get involved in the smallest details and to bless us in the simplest ways.

I trust that many will be inspired and blessed by the simple retelling of these simple stories of the miracles of God. May *The Little Book of Miracles* bring faith to your life and hope to you for a better tomorrow through faith in our Lord Jesus Christ.

Annie Hill Davis
Dudley, North Carolina

- 1 -

THE MIRACLE OF
THE LOST BOY
WHO CAME HOME

*And all things, whatsoever ye shall ask
in prayer, believing, ye shall receive.*
Matthew 21:22

A twelve-year-old boy in the state
of North Carolina began skipping school with
some of his friends. This got so bad that he
was threatened with expulsion. Then one day
his teacher called his home to say that the boy,
along with a friend, had run away. When his
mother heard this news, her heart was bro-

9

ken. She called on friends and family to try to find the boy, but they were unsuccessful.

The next day the boy's grandmother called to say that he had been seen with another grandson, a fourteen-year-old. He had apparently thumbed a ride about fifty miles to meet this cousin, and the two had been seen together, but now no one knew of their whereabouts.

It was believed that neither of the boys had any money, and neither of them had taken any extra clothes. How could they survive on their own?

But this mother believed in prayer and believed in the promises of God. She was sure that God meant what He said:

> *For with God nothing shall be impossible.*   Luke 1:37

She prayed and asked others to pray that God would protect the two runaway boys, would keep them safe, and would bring them back home. She expected to get a phone call any minute or to hear someone knock at the door with some news of her son. His photo appeared in the newspaper with the number to call if anyone saw him.

A week passed with no notice of the boys, then two weeks. With every passing day, it seemed less likely that anyone would hear from the boys, but this mother continued to believe for a miracle. Sometimes she stayed awake late into the night praying for her son, finally crying herself to sleep in the wee hours of the morning.

The boys were seen and recognized on several occasions and, when the mother got word of these sightings, she would rush to the indicated place, hoping to find her child at last. But by the time she got there, the boys had already moved on. To where, she had no idea.

Sometimes it was hard for the mother to get up and go to work in the morning. She hadn't been getting enough sleep recently, it was now three weeks, and she had no news of her son. When she thought she could not go on like this much longer, she remembered the promise of the Lord:

I can do all things through Christ which strengtheneth me.　　Philippians 4:13

She was sure that this was just a test of her faith and was determined to remain faithful. She was sure that God was faithful and that He would send her son home in His time. The delay did not mean that God was not hearing her prayer, nor that He would not eventually answer.

Like any mother, she was burdened for her son, but life had to go on; and, although it was hard for her not to spend her days in tears, she was able to do her assigned work.

She assured herself that if she had no problems she would have no need of God's help. He had allowed this to happen to see if she loved Him, and if she would trust Him, His promise was sure:

> *And we know that all things work together for good to them that love God, to them who are the called according to his purpose.*　　Romans 8:28

Annie Hill Davis

God would answer her prayers.

At work, one of the ladies told her about the trouble she was having with her own son. Every time he got a job he would work until payday, then take off, and spend his entire paycheck drinking. This always resulted in his being fired and the whole thing starting all over again.

He had been married and had three children, but his drinking had broken up the home, and he was now back living with his parents. His behavior so disturbed this mother that she got migraine headaches and had to take time off from work and visit a doctor, who treated her for her nerves.

The first mother began to tell the second about the love of God, insisting that God could save her son and deliver him from alcoholism. God could also deliver her from worrying about her son or anything else. He had promised:

> *Thou wilt keep him in perfect peace, whose mind is stayed on thee: because he trusteth in thee.* Isaiah 26:3

13

When the first mother made this declaration, she was suddenly assailed by the enemy of her soul. "You're saying that God can help this woman, but He hasn't helped you," he told her. "You're saying that God can save her son, but He hasn't saved yours yet. You're saying that God can answer her prayer, but He hasn't answered yours yet."

The woman refused to receive this attack, whispering, "Devil, you're a liar, and the truth is not to be found in you. Get behind me. I know that God can do all these things, and I believe that He will. So I will cling to His altar until the answer comes, for I know that it will come."

She could barely hold back her tears as she continued to challenge the other Christian lady. "Not only will God save your son," she told her, "God can save your husband, too, and I believe He will."

The second mother was a believer, although her husband was not, and she was more than ready to pray and believe God for a miracle. The two mothers agreed in prayer, believing God to hear and answer their respective needs. About a week later the friend came to work to say that God had saved her son and delivered him from alcohol. A few weeks after that God saved the husband. The son later got married to a Christian girl, and they are both serving the Lord.

God had not forgotten the first mother, either. About a month after her twelve-year-old son ran away, he came back home. The answer to her prayers had been delayed, but her faith had prevailed. She fully believed:

Now faith is the substance of things hoped for, the evidence of things not seen.

Hebrews 11:1

Just as she had asked Him to do, God had kept her son safe and brought him home again.

I know this to be a true story, for I was that mother. Thank You, Jesus, for performing a miracle on a lost son and bringing him home again. ❀

THE MIRACLE OF
A SON FORGIVEN

*Train up a child in the way he should go:
and when he is old, he will not depart
from it.*   Proverbs 22:6

I n the same state of North Carolina, a
seventeen-year-old boy started hanging out
with the wrong people and got in trouble
with the law· He was from a Christian home
and his mother believed the promise of God.

The boy was now confined in a youth cen-
ter many miles from home. His mother
prayed for him and asked others to pray for
him.

One evening when her husband came home from work he brought a letter from their son. From the letter it appeared that the charges against the boy were much more serious than they had believed. He was soon to be transferred to a jail in Goldsboro to stand trial for forgery. Each of the four charges against him carried a maximum penalty of twenty years of imprisonment.

The Lord spoke to the mother to fast for en days and to pray for her son. She knew the voice of God and believed that God would move on her son's behalf if she obeyed Him. She told the whole family that she would not be eating for the next ten days. She loved God and her son more than food. She requested prayer in her church and from her friends as well.

One night, during a local tent revival, the minister said to the people gathered that God was ready to give them whatever it was they were believing for at the moment. If they would stand to their feet and dance before the Lord in faith, He would do the work. That mother believed what was being said, so she stood to her feet and began to dance and praise God, thanking Him in advance for answering her prayer. Then, she put the entire matter out of her mind. She was at rest in her faith in God.

The morning of the scheduled trial, she took off from work to attend. She called the Goldsboro jail to see if her son had arrived there yet, and when she was told that he hadn't, she was concerned because it was only an hour until his trial was due to begin. When she called the courthouse to inquire, she was told that all the charges against her son had been dismissed.

After hanging up the phone, she thought probably there had been some mistake. Maybe there was another accused by the same name. So she decided to call back and inquire further. She had been right the first time she was told. It was indeed her son, and the charges against him had been dismissed.

"What do you mean by 'dismissed'?" she asked the court secretary.

The lady answered, "Let me connect you to the judge, and let him explain it to you."

Annie Hill Davis

The judge said that 'dismissed' meant that the charges had been dropped. They could be reinstituted anytime within the next two years, but, for now at least, her son was cleared. If two years passed and nothing further was filed, no further charges could be brought. The Lord now reminded her that she had fasted and prayed and that others had believed with her for her son's release, and God had answered their prayers.

As it turned out, the lawyer who had filed the warrants was moved by the son's repentance and his promise to pay back the money and to do better in the future. But who could doubt that it was God who moved on his heart in response to the determined prayers of his mother and others?

This was also a true story. I know, for I am that mother. Thank You, Jesus, for the miracle of a son forgiven.   ❈

THE MIRACLE OF
A MOTHER'S
DYING WISHES

Honour thy father and thy mother: that thy days may be long upon the land which the LORD thy God giveth thee.

Exodus 20:12

During the summer of 1976, my sister and her husband decided to move to Texas. Our father had died of tuberculosis in February of the year before, and Mother wondered if she would ever see my sister and brother-in-law again. She gave them Christmas presents before they left that summer. As it turned out, Mama was right. She died on the first day of December of that year.

Mama had somehow foreseen this event and had given Christmas presents early to every member of the family. She had laid away a watch for one grandson that later had to be picked up, but everything else was personally presented. How she knew that her time had come no one could say for sure. She just knew.

One granddaughter was living with her at the time, and one grandson lived just a few doors away, but two weeks before she died Mother came to my house and spent the night with me. She was going away to spend a week with her sister and another week with my brother and, for some reason, she felt that she might never return to her own home again.

I encouraged her to do whatever she wanted. She had nothing to tie her down. Why not spend a week or two with each of her children if she wanted to?

I later learned that she had told the granddaughter living with her that if anything happened to her, she wanted me to have the flag that had been given to her when my brother, David, died in an air crash while on duty in the Pacific. I still have that flag.

She had designated one son to get her freezer and a grandson to have her mobile home because he had come into some money from his father's accidental death and had finished paying for the home when his granddaddy died.

When Mama got back home after her two visits, she somehow didn't expect to live long, and that same day she began to experience chest pains. They were so severe that my niece alerted Mother's doctor. He told her that if Mama began to vomit she would know that it was a heart attack, and she should get her to the emergency room immediately.

Mama went outside in the fresh air and sat on the porch step, but before long she began to vomit, and my nephew called to say that my niece was rushing her to the emergency room. Although I didn't want to believe it, I sensed that God was calling my mother home.

About a mile from the hospital my niece had a flat tire on her car. She got out and flagged down a passing motorist who took them the rest of the way to the hospital. As soon as the doctors saw my mother's condition, they placed her in the intensive care unit.

She was permitted only two visitors every two hours for five minutes, so I didn't get in to see her until 2:00 in the morning. They had tubes going into her nose and other machines hooked up to her. She told me that her eyes and chest hurt, and I prayed with her.

When I went back to the intensive care unit two hours later, Mother seemed to be much better. I prayed with her again and started to leave, telling her that she needed to get some rest and that I would see her at 6:00. But she wasn't sure. "I don't think I'm going to be here much longer," she said.

At the time I thought she meant she wouldn't have to stay much longer in the hospital. She was in good spirits and wanted to talk about her visit with her sister and my brother and his family. She had really enjoyed seeing everyone.

When 6:00 came and no one called me for visiting hours, I knew something was wrong. When I tried to go through the swinging doors at the nurses' station, a nurse blocked my way. "You'll have to go back to the waiting room," she said. "We will call you."

I saw nurses and doctors running toward the intensive care unit. Mama had died at exactly 6:00 in the morning of a massive heart attack. Her doctor appeared in a few minutes to give us the news.

We didn't have an address for my sister and her family who had moved to Texas, and when we tried to locate them, we were unable to do so. We prayed that God would help us to contact them in time for the funeral. When more time passed and the viewing was to be held the very next day, our prayers reached serious intensity.

I was sitting on my couch next to the telephone praying about this matter when it rang. It was a Christian lady friend of mine I hadn't seen for several days. We attended the same church, and I had asked her to pray that God would send my sister home before the funeral. "I just wanted to tell you," she said now, "that the Lord gave me a vision of you. You were sitting on the couch next to the phone."

She described to me the clothing I was wearing at that very moment and said that she saw Jesus sitting beside me with His arms around me. He was telling me not to worry, that everything was going to be all right, and that my sister would be there before the funeral.

As she described to me this vision, I could feel the power and presence of God there with me, and I believed that God was indeed going to do a miracle for us.

The next night we all went to the funeral home for the viewing and then back to my brother's house where all the family had agreed to meet. No one had yet heard from our sister, but I assured them that she would be there on time. No more than ten minutes had gone by when she and her family arrived. In all the flurry of activity, I never did learn how she had gotten word of our mother's death, but I knew that God had done a miracle, and I was grateful to Him. It didn't matter whom He had used.

My sister told me that a week or two before Mama died God had spoken to her to take her picture off the wall, anoint it with oil, and claim her soul, and she had obeyed God. Thank You, Jesus, for the miracle of a mother's dying wishes. ❀

4

THE MIRACLE OF RECEIVING THE DESIRES OF OUR HEARTS

Delight thyself also in the LORD; and he
shall give thee the desires of thine heart.
Commit thy way unto the LORD; trust
also in him; and he shall bring it to pass.
Psalms 37:4-5

The Friday before Mother's Day of
1997, I was sitting in my living room reading
when I realized that I was hungry for some
good country ham. I had no sooner laid down
the book I was reading than there was a knock

at the door. It was my son, Bobby, with his daughter, Christi, and they had brought me a gift of a country ham with a Mother's Day card attached.

Praise God, for He will give us the desires of our hearts. He has promised:

> *For the LORD God is a sun and shield:*
> *the LORD will give grace and glory: no*
> *good thing will he withhold from them*
> *that walk uprightly.* Psalms 84:11

God knows our very thoughts and is concerned about us. As He has promised, He will not withhold any good thing from us when we love Him. Praise His Holy name. Thank You, Jesus, for giving us the very desires of our hearts. ❂

5

THE MIRACLE OF
A VACATION IN FLORIDA

For with God nothing shall be impossible.
Luke 1:37

One day in the summer of 1982, God spoke to me at my place of work and told me to plan a visit to my daughter, Sue, in Homestead, Florida. Although I knew God was speaking to me, I didn't have the money to go to Florida, and I wasn't sure I could get enough time off from work. When I mentioned these problems to the Lord, He told me to take $50 out of each week's paycheck until I had enough to make the trip. I didn't see how I could do that, but I knew if God said I should go, I would be able to afford it.

When I told my husband, John, about my plan, he wasn't at all excited about it. He said he couldn't afford to miss a week from work because we needed the money. I said that I could take Brenda, our twelve-year-old daughter, and explained to him that it had been quite a while since we had seen Sue and her family, so I knew she must be just as anxious to see us as we were to see them.

John wondered if I should try to drive that far since I had never driven more than two hundred miles in my life and this was a six-teen-hundred-mile trip. He suggested that, if we did insist on going, we should take a bus. I felt that God had told me to drive, so I knew that we would be fine and not get lost, but I wanted my husband to feel good about our going.

One night I had a dream in which I saw myself and Brenda approaching an empty house. It was night, and there was a large black dog chained to a stake in the ground in the front yard. As we passed the dog, he began to bark and jump at us and did this until he broke the chain and came after us. He grabbed my right hand in his teeth and wouldn't let go. Brenda clung to my other hand.

In the dream, I was afraid to move for fear that the dog would tear the flesh from my hand or break a bone. All I knew to do was to start praising the Lord. As I praised Him, the animal began to loosen his grip a little at a time. I kept on praising the Lord until the dog at last let go of me completely and ran to the house.

I wasn't sure what the dream meant, so I asked the Lord. He told me that the dog's teeth represented Satan's efforts to keep me from making the trip to Florida. But just as I had praised God until the teeth of the dog let loose of my hand, I should praise Him until a way was made for me to make this trip.

From that day on, I left everything in His hands, and just trusted Him, and rejoiced, knowing that He would make a way. I did, however, have conflicting feelings about the trip. I knew that God had told me to go, but I didn't want to do it unless John was in complete agreement. I decided not to mention it to him again, but just to pray.

The devil tried everything to stop me from making that trip. John's car was parked in a low spot at a mill, and a sudden flood came and damaged the car so that it had to be put in the shop. He now had no way to get back and forth to work, and the shop where he took his car told him it would not be fixed until the following week. I was believing the Lord to leave on Saturday morning, so I prayed that his car would be fixed by Friday instead. I was believing the promise of God: *"For with God nothing shall be impossible."* On Friday the repair shop called to say the car was ready, so one hindrance to our going was removed.

I was so sure we were going that I wanted to buy some snacks and drinks to take with us on the highway, but by Friday my husband hadn't mentioned the trip for several days, so I waited. I worked that day from 6:30 in the morning until 2:30 in the afternoon, and he had to work from 2:30 in the afternoon until 10:30 at night, so there didn't seem to be time even for us to talk about the trip. But when he got to our place of work, he asked me, "Have you got any drinks and snacks to take with you yet?"

"No," I said, "I hadn't bought anything because you haven't said we could go yet."

"Well, I got some things for you," he said. "It's all at the house waiting."

All I could do was praise the Lord. God had not only changed his mind but had caused him to buy the things we needed along the way.

I went home and packed our clothes. I had waited to do it until I knew it was all right with my husband. I knew that God would work it out, and he did. He is never late. He is always on time. Brenda and I had a wonderful time in Florida. Sue took us to the Miami Zoo, the Miami Sea Aquarium, and Disney World, and paid all of our expenses.

Thank You, Jesus, for the miracle of a vacation in Florida.   ❖

6

THE MIRACLE OF
THE $100 BLESSING

*And they rose early in the morning, and
went forth into the wilderness of Tekoa:
and as they went forth, Jehoshaphat stood
and said, Hear me, O Judah, and ye in-
habitants of Jerusalem; Believe in the
LORD your God, so shall ye be estab-
lished; believe his prophets, so shall ye
prosper.* 2 Chronicles 20:20

My sister and her husband, both
preachers, came to my house one day to visit.
Before they left we all joined hands and
prayed, and after we finished praying my

brother-in-law told me that the Lord was going to bless me with $100 within a week. I believed God's prophet and praised Him for that promise.

Sure enough, within a week someone gave me a hundred dollar bill. Strangely enough, I had forgotten all about what my brother-in-law said until after I received the money. Then the Lord reminded me of the day we had prayed together and the promise He had given me through His prophet.

That was the first time anyone had ever given me $100. If we believe God's prophets we are destined to prosper. God knows what we need, when we need it, and how to bring it to us.

Thank You, Jesus, for the miracle of the $100 blessing.   ❀

7

THE MIRACLE OF
THE LOST DOCUMENT

*But the Comforter, which is the Holy
Ghost, whom the Father will send in my
name, he shall teach you all things, and
bring all things to your remembrance,
whatsoever I have said unto you.*

John 14:26

My son-in-law, Matthew, had a vision when he was only five years old. He later wrote it down and, because it blessed me so much when I read it, he gave me a copy. I treasured it and put it away for safekeeping.

Sometimes, when I was alone, I would get it out and read it and get blessed all over again.

Then, one day when my daughter and grandchildren had come from Florida to visit us, she told me that something had happened to their copy of the vision. They couldn't find it, and Matthew was very distressed about it. She had forgotten that he had given me a copy, so I reminded her. I would get out my copy, I told her.

When I went to look for my copy of the vision, it, too, was missing. I was sure that I had just misplaced it, but when the day came for them to return to Florida, I still hadn't been able to find it. I told my daughter that I would keep looking for it and would send it to them as soon as I found it.

Several weeks went by, and I was praying seriously one day about that vision. God knows all things, and I was sure He could bring to my remembrance what I had done with that paper. I was claiming the promise of His Word.

I had searched through several old purses three or four times each, thinking that I might have left it in one of them. I looked in my brief case and filing cabinet several times and even in my safety deposit box at the bank. The paper could not be found in any of those places. *Well,* I thought, *I'm tired of thinking about it right now. I believe I'll just lie down across the bed and take a little nap. I'll look for it again later.*

I hadn't laid there very long before the Lord impressed me to get up and look in the filing cabinet again. I thought to myself, *I already looked there many times and didn't find it,* but I felt the Lord was speaking to me, so I had to obey. I jumped out of bed, picked up the small filing cabinet, and took it into the living room.

There I poured everything that was in it out on the floor and began to search through it. Much to my surprise, there was the paper I was looking for. It just seemed to jump out at me so easily. I quickly called Sue to tell her I had found it, then I made a copy of it and sent it to them.

I had put the paper in a special envelope that would protect it and had forgotten what it was in and exactly where I had placed it, but the Lord knew. I believe that He knows all things, and if we are doing something that brings Him glory, He will help us when our memory is lacking.

God knew that Matthew would lose his copy and that's why a second copy was given to me. God knew that I would treasure it, that it would bless me, and that I would keep it safe until it was needed.

I thank God for Matthew and Sue. They have been married for about eighteen years now and have two beautiful daughters, Heather and Krystle. I thank God for the vision Matthew had and for his willingness to share it with me. I still treasure my copy of it and am blessed when I read it.

Thank You, Jesus, for the miracle of the lost document.   ✸

THE MIRACLE OF THE FORGOTTEN PHONE CONVERSATION

Behold, I am the LORD, the God of all flesh: is there any thing too hard for me?
Jeremiah 32:27

One afternoon I was sitting in my living room when the phone rang. It was my dentist's office reminding me of an upcoming appointment. While we were talking, my husband called to me from the back door. "Come out here quickly," he said, and I could tell from the tone of his voice that something was wrong. I finished my conversation quickly, hung up, and rushed outside.

There stood one of my next-door neighbors. She had just gotten a call that her mother, who had been visiting with her for a few days, had fallen in Hardees and broken her hip, and had been taken to the hospital. This neighbor didn't drive and wondered if I could take her to the hospital. I told her I would be glad to.

As she went off to get ready to go, my husband asked me, "Who was that on the phone?" and I was amazed to find that I couldn't remember who I had been talking to only a moment before. With the shock of my neighbor's sudden appearance at my door, my mind had suddenly gone blank.

"You're not going to believe this," I answered, "but I don't remember who was on the phone or what we were talking about." How could I expect him to believe that? I could hardly believe it either and found it to be a scary feeling. It was the first time such a thing had ever happened to me, and I hoped it would be the last.

"I'll pray about it," I told my husband, "and I'm sure the Lord will bring it back to my remembrance."

I took my neighbor to the hospital and, on the way, we talked about the Lord. I told her my unusual experience and that I was believing God to bring back to my remembrance who I had been talking to and why.

When I got back home, my husband asked me if I had remembered yet. I had to admit that I didn't, but I was sure that I would.

Several hours later, after my husband had gone to bed, I was sitting in the living room reading my Bible when suddenly it came back to me. I rushed to the bedroom to tell my husband the good news, only to find that he was sleeping already. I was so happy for what the Lord had done that I just couldn't keep the news to myself. I woke him up and told him about it.

We can trust the Lord to help us in our moments of distress. Thank You, Jesus, for the miracle of the forgotten phone conversation.   ❈

- 9 -

THE MIRACLE OF HEALING FROM SPINAL MENINGITIS

But he was wounded for our transgressions, he was bruised for our iniquities: the chastisement of our peace was upon him; and with his stripes we are healed.

Isaiah 53:5

My grandson, Joshua, was born on the first day of August in 1986, and the Lord gave him a miracle when he was just three months old. He became very ill with a high fever and had to be taken to a doctor. When

43

he got to the doctor's office, they found his fever to be 105° or more. A spinal tap revealed that he had spinal meningitis, and he was quickly admitted to the Wayne Memorial Hospital in Goldsboro.

When I got the news, I began to pray and fast for his healing. I had heard of several cases of spinal meningitis in children which had resulted in death or permanent brain damage. One lady told me that her brother had suffered the same thing, and it left him with permanent ear damage.

I called our pastors at the time, James and Fannie Davis (who just happened to be my sister and brother-in-law) and asked them to pray for him. Our church was having a revival with Sister Anne Baines, and everyone present prayed for Joshua that night.

God answered prayer. Although Joshua stayed in the hospital a total of ten days, he began to improve from that first day, and he was left with no long-term consequences of the illness.

In fact, Joshua is now an intelligent kindergarten student. He knows his ABC's, can count to a hundred, can write complete sentences, and can spell many words. He has known all the books of the New Testament by memory since he was four.

Pat Rayburn, my niece, was his Sunday school teacher for a time. She was a wonderful teacher, and during the time that she taught them, all the children loved her very much and responded to her teaching.

One Sunday morning she asked me if I had been teaching Joshua the books of the Bible. He was staying with me some, and I would always take him to church when his parents were unable to go, but I hadn't been able specifically to teach him the books of the Bible, and I told her so.

She said that she had been surprised when some of the older children were reciting the names of the books that Joshua had wanted to do it too. She wondered how far he would get but told him to go ahead. To her surprise, he knew them all. I had helped him some and his mother had helped him, too, but he had learned mostly by sitting and listening to the older children. Praise God, Joshua was not only healed, but was blessed with a good mind. To God be all the glory.

Joshua still loves the Lord and still loves to go to church. When the invitation is given for those who want prayer, he always goes forward. He wants more and more of God. Every time I look at him, I realize that I am seeing a living miracle. Thank You, Jesus, for the miracle of healing from meningitis. ❇

10

THE MIRACLE OF SURVIVING A SERIOUS ACCIDENT

And all mine are thine, and thine are mine; and I am glorified in them.

John 17:10

Our son, Jimmy, had a 1980 Mazda, and one night when he was going around a sharp curve, he lost control of the car, and it rolled over five times. He was thrown from the car onto the highway, and he rolled over and over for a long distance, too.

The car went down into a ditch and across

a field. When I saw it later and took pictures of it, I couldn't believe how horribly it was smashed up. It was a total loss.

But God did a great miracle for Jimmy. He suffered some minor cuts and abrasions on his back, legs, and arms, but he got up and walked away from the accident. Before long, he was completely well. Praise God.

Jimmy had not been wearing a seat belt, but he did have an anointed prayer cloth in the pocket of that car. I had been praying and standing in the gap for him and had others praying for him also. God had His hand on Jimmy's life, and Satan could not kill him.

Jesus said all that is ours is His, as well. Our families—children and grandchildren—and even our friends are protected by our prayers. Thank You, Jesus, for the miracle of Jimmy surviving a serious accident.   ❋

11

THE MIRACLE OF GOD KNOWING OUR THOUGHTS

For there is nothing hid, which shall not be manifested; neither was any thing kept secret, but that it should come abroad.

Mark 4:22

For two years I had been wanting to attend the Ladies Convention at the Calvary Pentecostal Campground in Ashland, Virginia. Having heard of the good things God was doing there, I wanted to experience it for myself. The problem was that I just didn't have the money to go.

Then, one day someone called to say that they had been led to pay all my expenses—registration, hotel and meals—to attend the convention and had already taken the liberty of registering my name. They hoped I didn't mind. Mind? It was an answer to prayer. My sister, Mildred, and I went together and had a wonderful time in the excellent anointed services there.

Praise God, for He is concerned about us. He will make a way when it seems there is no way. Nothing is impossible with Him.

Thank You, Jesus, for the miracle of Your knowing our every thought and desire.   ✾

12

THE MIRACLE OF A TRIP TO ISRAEL

And Jesus looking upon them saith, With men it is impossible, but not with God: for with God all things are possible.

Mark 10:27

About ten years ago, I made a prayer list one day, writing down all the things I wanted God to do for me. One of the things I wrote there was that I wanted to go to Israel. That would require a great miracle, because there was no way in this world I could afford to go on a trip like that.

Several years passed, and one day someone handed me $300 and said, "This is on your trip to Israel."

I said, "Well, I don't know when I'll ever be able to go, but I'll put the money in the bank and keep it until I can go."

The fact that someone would give me money and designate it for that trip caused me to sense that God was going to do the miracle, and I began to believe Him for it. How would He do it? I didn't know, but I was sure that He would put it on the heart of someone to help me. I put the money in the bank and, after a while, put the whole matter out of my mind.

Then one day in the summer of 1992, the Lord spoke to me and told me that it was time to go that fall with a group from the Calvary Camp. "I send thee," He said. I wanted to believe what the Lord was saying, but I knew that the cost of the trip was $2,220, and I didn't have that kind of money to spare. If I borrowed the money to go, I felt I wouldn't be able to make the payments on it. What should I do? God had said that He was going to send me.

First, I wanted to be sure this message was from God. I mentioned it to my husband, and his response was as expected, "You know you don't have the money, and you can't pay it back if you borrow it." I knew he was right, and the enemy used that to discourage me and make me doubt that the whole idea was of God.

I loved going to the Ashland campground and had been going every summer since 1974. It was well worth the time. There were preachers from all over the world who came together for nine or ten weeks during the summer months. I had been blessed there so many times that, as I thought about it now, I was sure what God had told me there must be true. I needed to go to the Holy Land.

Since only $200 was required in advance to make a reservation for the trip, I decided to take that much from the bank and sign up for the trip—in faith that God would provide what was lacking. When I got to camp, however, the enemy worked me over so thoroughly that I began to doubt again that my going to Israel was of the Lord. Where would

I get the rest of the money? If God wanted me to go, I decided, He could have someone put even the $200 deposit in my hands or to pay it directly to the tour office. Of course, that was a foolish mistake. God had already given me $300, and He would provide the rest—if I would only believe Him.

After I had disobeyed in this regard, God told me to give $100 to the camp, $100 to the speaker that week, and, what's more, to give $50 to my pastor for his trip (whenever he wanted to go) and $50 for his wife. In very short order, I was left with no money saved for the trip.

I said, "Lord, I have obeyed You in giving, and now I have nothing toward my trip. I will have to trust You fully. Help me."

The next week we went back to camp for several more days. I was seeking God for a sign to let me know His will for October when one of the lady missionaries approached me in an outdoor patio and began to prophesy over me. "Do what I have told you to do," the Lord said. "It is I that have put it into your heart and not you yourself. I will send you."

She prayed for Brenda, too. Brenda wanted to go with me on the trip, but she didn't have any money either. The Lord spoke to her, "I have put it in thy heart to go, and I will make the way."

Brenda was working as a waitress in a restaurant at the time and didn't know if she could even get off work or not. At the very least, she would have to get someone to work in her place.

That night after the service we were standing around the altar praying, and the preacher called me out and said he wanted to pray for me. He spoke a word of prophesy over me also. He didn't know me, didn't know anything about my wanting to go to Israel, and didn't know what I was praying about at the time. Yet, he was led to say, "Don't back up, don't back up. Do what I have told thee. I will send thee. Thou hast stood back and prayed for others to go and said, 'I'll go later,' but I say, now is the time."

I had an assurance, from that day on, that I would make the trip, although I still didn't know how God would do it. He would make a way.

"Brenda," I told my daughter, "I don't have any assurance about you. You may have to pay your own way or borrow the money to go, but I know that God is going to send me. I have no more doubts."

Brenda was able to borrow enough to pay her way and would pay it back at $100 a month with no interest. After she got her money that way, I decided that I could believe God to pay back $100 a month, so I did the same thing.

I had my fare, now I just needed some spending money. I would want to buy some souvenirs for my family and friends. I was believing God for $300. I had obeyed Him in giving $300 to others, and I knew that He would be faithful to me.

My husband was concerned about my not having any spending money, so he gave me $100 about a week before I was to leave. I bought a sweater I would need for the trip and took my son and his family out to eat. When he heard about it, my husband was understandably upset. He said, "You won't have any money to spend on the trip."

"I will," I answered, "the Lord is going to give me $300 before I leave."

"Well, I want to see that," He said.

"Okay," I replied, "you will."

Mildred decided to accompany us on the trip. When the day came for us to go to Ashland camp and join the team, I still didn't have the money I was believing for. She and I and Brenda and John ate breakfast together at Shoney's that day before we left for Ashland, and John said to me, "Do you need me to give you some more money? You won't have enough."

I accepted his offer but assured him that God was going to give me enough to make up the $300 I needed. "Even if He doesn't," I assured him, "I'll be fine."

Someone paid for our breakfast and gave me five dollars. We went out, said our good-byes, got in our respective cars, and John started backing his car out to go on home. We were just about to leave when someone put an envelope in my hands and, when I opened it, I found $300—my spending money.

I couldn't get the window down fast enough to catch John before he started off, so we went after him and kept motioning for him to stop. When he did, I held up the money, saying, "I told you I would have $300. Now I have $400, including the $100 you gave me." He just smiled and drove off.

God had done what He promised to do. He had wanted to see if I was willing to give away all I had and to trust Him for the rest and, when I did, He gave me back $100 more than I had given.

It was a wonderful trip. More than the best vacation I ever had, it was an education. I had told Mildred that if I was able to go once, I would never again want to spend that much money to go again. She had already been to the Holy Land five or six times. But after I went, I knew why she wanted to go back. I wanted to go back, too, and I believe I will someday.

About two weeks before my first payment was due on the money I had borrowed, I got $100 in the mail from someone who said that it was for my trip to Israel. Later, someone gave me an envelope, saying that they had been told to give it to me and not to tell me where it came from. When I opened the envelope, I found five $100 bills.

"What am I supposed to do with it?" I asked the person.

"Put it on your trip to Israel," they replied.

I had already felt that was what I was supposed to do with it.

Later still, Brenda came home from work one day with an envelope someone had handed her for me. It contained $100 which she was told was for my trip to Israel. We never knew who gave it, but it didn't matter. God was supplying my need.

As the money came in by this miraculous means, I was able to pay off my indebtedness in less than eight months, and Brenda paid hers off as well. We considered that our trip was well worth the money. We would never forget the trip and would never be the same again.

Thank You, Jesus, for the miracle of a trip to Israel.   ❊

13

THE MIRACLE OF JOSHUA'S NEW SHOES

Jesus said unto him, If thou canst believe, all things are possible to him that believeth.   Mark 9:23

I t was nearly time for school to start one fall, and Joshua would be in the second grade. He had some shoes, but they were old, and he needed some new ones. He had a bookbag, but it was old, too, and he needed a new one. His parents didn't have money to get those two items before school would start, but I told him, "Let's pray and ask the Lord to make a way for you to get what you need before school starts." So we prayed.

A few days later I went to the mailbox to see if we had any mail and found that someone had put an envelope in there. It had no stamp on it and had not come through the mail. It was addressed to me, so I opened it, to find $50 and a note that read:

"Take this money and go buy Joshua a nice pair of shoes and a bookbag. If there is any money left over, give it to him."

There was no signature.

It was more than enough money to buy the shoes and the bookbag, and I gave the rest to Joshua.

We pondered that miracle for a very long time. We hadn't told anybody about Joshua's need, but someone had listened to the voice of God and had been unwilling to take the credit for the gift. Thank You, Jesus, for the miracle of Joshua's new shoes. ❋

14

THE MIRACLE OF
AN ANOINTED
PRAYER CLOTH

*And God wrought special miracles by the
hands of Paul: So that from his body were
brought unto the sick handkerchiefs or
aprons, and the diseases departed from
them, and the evil spirits went out of
them.* Acts 19:11-12

In January of 1996, we had a healing
service at our church in Pikeville. It was or-
dained by God and many miracles were received. Rev. Wayne Goff was the speaker that

day. After he preached, we had a prayer line. I got in the line and got some prayer cloths and had him anoint them and pray over them. My intention was to give them to certain people that God had laid on my heart. Rev. Goff prayed over the cloths—for the physical, spiritual, and financial needs of those who would receive them, for the healing of their souls, and for the protection of their automobiles.

I was led to give one of those anointed cloths to my brother who lived about sixty miles away. I went to his house a few days later to give it to him, only to find that he wasn't home.

I wasn't able to return until four or five weeks later, and when I did, I found my brother in bed. He got up, but he was experiencing a lot of pain in one of his lungs. Once before this had happened to his other lung and he had to have fluid drawn off of it.

I asked him how long he had been sick, and he said, "For awhile now."

"Has it been as long as five weeks?" I asked.

"Yes, it has," he replied. "Why do you say that?"

I told him how I had felt led to get a prayer cloth anointed and prayed over for him during the healing service at our church and how I had come to give it to him, but he hadn't been home. I had felt led, now, to come again and bring it to him.

I took it out of my purse then, walked over to his chair, and put it in the pocket over that lung where he was suffering. I intended to pray for him, and I stood there beside his chair a few minutes waiting for everyone to stop talking so I could do it. But they kept on talking, so I went back and sat down.

I felt badly about not praying for my brother because I knew God had put it in my heart to do it. That's why I had gone there in the first place.

A few minutes later he felt in his pocket and asked, "Where did you put the cloth? I can't find it." That gave me another opportunity. I got up and walked over to his chair. I took the cloth out of his pocket and showed it to him, then put it back in his pocket.

"I'm not hurting as bad as before you put it in there," he said.

I put my hand on him, in the spot he said he was hurting, and told everyone present, "Let's pray for him." I asked God to help him and to take away all the pain. I wanted him to tell me before I left that he had stopped hurting altogether.

We stayed about thirty more minutes, and when I got ready to leave I told him we would keep on praying for him. He told me that he had stopped hurting altogether, and that he felt much better.

I had given prayer cloths to two of my sons. One of them, within a few weeks, received more than $3,000 and the other received nearly that much.

It always pays to obey God, and when we don't we are missing a blessing or cause someone else to miss theirs. If we fail to obey, God will always use someone else whom He can trust, but we don't want to lose those opportunities.

We should listen to the voice of God when He speaks to us to pray for someone, to go see someone, to speak with someone on the phone or anything else He tells us to do. And we should waste no time in doing it.

Thank You, Jesus, for the miracle of an anointed prayer cloth. ✸

15

THE MIRACLE OF
COMING HOME

*Likewise, I say unto you, there is joy in
the presence of the angels of God over one
sinner that repenteth.*   Luke 15:10

W hile working one day in the factory, I became very burdened for my son and his family. They had once served God, but had gone back. I had been fasting and praying for them. As I thought about their situation now, I became so burdened that I went to the bathroom to be alone and pray more effectively. No one else was there, so I lifted my voice and cried out to God.

The Little Book of Miracles

In those moments, God gave me a vision. I saw my son and his family living in a mobile home. It was raining, and my son came out the door and started walking down the road in the rain. His hands hung limply at his side.

Soon, I saw his wife come out and begin walking down the road behind him. Next, the older son came out and walked down the road behind his mother. Then the younger son came out and walked down the road behind his brother. They all walked along in silence as it began to rain harder, and the sky filled with thunder and lightning.

After the family had walked several blocks, they all stopped and turned around. There seemed to be an equal distance between them as they stood in the rain. Then, the thunder and lightning stopped, and the rain stopped, and the family walked back toward their home.

I heard the voice of God saying, "They will come," and the vision ended.

I opened my eyes and, before I went back out to work, took time to thank God for speaking to me in this way. He had heard my cry and was giving me an answer.

I felt that God had shown the family's recent history. As they walked away from home, they were really walking away from God and from His house. The storms of life seemed to bring them to their senses, and they had turned and made a decision to go back home. Their decision had changed things for them, and the storm had ceased.

When God said to me, "They will come," I felt that He meant they would be soon coming back to him. That was all I needed to hear. I was thrilled and rejoiced in the promise of God.

That weekend, my son and his family all came back to God, just as God had shown me. Thank You, Jesus, for the miracle of coming home.   ✺

16

THE MIRACLE OF INTERCESSORY PRAYER

*Again I say unto you, That if two of you
shall agree on earth as touching any thing
that they shall ask, it shall be done for
them of my Father which is in heaven.*

Matthew 18:19

As I lay in my bed one night thinking about Jesus and what He had done for me, I had a vision. I saw a girl with long hair, but I couldn't tell who she was because her back was toward me.

There was a huge, round net over the girl's

head. It was white and looked to be about ten or twelve feet wide, reaching to the ground on either side of her. She was struggling, trying with all her might to tear the net or to get free of it, but she could not.

Then, I watched as a figure dressed in a white robe came flying like a bird out of the sky. He was pointing to the girl's head, and as he drew near her, the net split and dropped to the ground all around her.

He came to earth beside her, took her hand, and said to her, "Will you follow Me? If you will, everything will be all right."

In that moment I knew that the girl I was seeing in the vision was my own niece. The enemy had tied her down, and she had been unable to get free from his net. But God was telling her that if she would follow Him He would help her. I sensed that God's purpose in showing me this was so that I could intercede for her in prayer.

I requested prayer for her at our church that God would reveal to her what he wanted her to do, and that she would obey.

I wasn't aware that she had been going

through such a difficult trial. She related to me later that the enemy had told her that there was no way out and that she should just end her life, once and for all. God was faithful, however, and showed her that if she would just put her trust in Him, He would make her victorious. He showed her exactly what to do, and she did come through that ordeal victoriously.

Thank You, Jesus, for the miracle of intercessory prayer.   ✳

17

THE MIRACLE OF GOD'S PROTECTION

God is our refuge and strength, a very present help in trouble. Psalms 46:1

My son, Bobby, and his family live only about a half mile from me, and I enjoyed taking walks with my grandchildren—Joshua (10) and Christi (7)—until my feet and legs began to bother me. Then I quit walking for a while.

One day the grandchildren called and asked me to walk over and get them and bring them back to my house. I didn't feel up to it, so I told them to ask their mother if they could walk over by themselves. I would be watching for them from the window. She agreed, and they came over.

When the two grandchildren got to my house, I asked them if they had seen any dogs on the way. A certain dog would often come out and bark at us as we went by. They said they hadn't seen any.

They stayed for about thirty minutes and, before they left, I called their mother to say they were on their way home and that she should be looking for them. Before long, however, Joshua came running back up on my porch crying, and a black dog was pulling at his pants legs.

Grand-Daddy John went out and chased the dog away. I assured Joshua that the dog was not trying to hurt him. If it had wanted to bite him, it would have done that already. It was just playing, but Joshua wasn't so sure. He was frightened.

"Where's Christi?" I asked him.

"She's back there on the next street," he said.

"Well, we'd better go get her," I said. "She must be scared to death to be left alone like that."

As I got the van to go after Christi, I was praying that the dog would not bite her on its way back home.

When we found her, she was standing as straight as a statue, with her hands at her side, crying as hard as she could. She was too terrified to move.

"Did the dog bite you?" I asked

"No," she sobbed.

"Then what happened?"

"When he came after me barking, I held out the cup of Mountain Dew you gave us. I said, 'Here, Dogie, here's some Mountain Dew. It's good, and you can have it.' " She had thrown the cup of Mountain Dew on the ground, and the dog had been distracted licking up the ice and the soda and forgot about barking at her for the moment. He had not forgotten her, however, and after he had licked up all the soda he stood there for a very long while watching her closely. That's why she was frozen in place when we found her.

The Little Book of Miracles

But God had protected both the children and had given Christi wisdom to know what to do in that situation. God has angels watching over His children. Thank You, Jesus, for Your protection.   ✸

18

THE MIRACLE OF
THE GUARDIAN ANGEL

*For he shall give his angels charge over
thee, to keep thee in all thy ways.*

Psalms 91:11

One very cold winter day in 1977, we
traveled to Rocky Mount, North Carolina, to
visit my sister and her family who lived there.
The pond in their yard was covered with ice,
and, while we visited inside, the children
went out to play around it. Brenda was seven
at the time, Bobby was twelve, and their
cousin, Janet, was thirteen.

Bobby and Janet convinced Brenda to walk way out on the ice, not realizing that there were thin spots where she could fall through and be drowned. The amazing thing is not that she fell through the ice, but that the others were somehow able to get her out and bring her in the house.

She was wet and cold, but I starting thanking God immediately for sparing her life. Pulling someone out of the ice is dangerous and difficult—even for trained adults, let alone children.

That night, after we got home, we went to church. A good Christian lady of the church, a friend of mine, said to us, "While I was praying this afternoon, I had a vision of Brenda." She described what Brenda was wearing at the time and how she had seen her fall into the water.

"She was going under," she continued, "when I saw an angel taking hold of her with hands and lifting her out of the water. I started praying for her."

"My God," I answered, "that's exactly what happened. God knew that Brenda would fall through the ice and had you praying and interceding for her.

Because God is so faithful to put it in the hearts of others to pray for us in our hour of need, we must each be faithful to intercede for those the Lord places upon our hearts. This is the way He does His miracles.

Thank You, Jesus, for the miracle of the guardian angel.   ❋

19

THE MIRACLE OF
GOD MAKING A WAY

*And all things, whatsoever ye shall ask
in prayer, believing, ye shall receive.*

Matthew 21:22

One Sunday morning while I was sitting in church the Lord put it in my heart to give five dollars to a certain lady who was there. I had my money tightly budgeted and knew that I had just enough to pay my bills that week, so I said, "Lord, You know I don't have any money except my bill money, because You know all things." He knew what I had, and He knew that I needed it, but He wanted to see if I would obey Him and trust Him to supply my need.

When He kept dealing with me to give it, I agreed—with one stipulation. "Okay, Lord," I said, "if You want me to give that money to her, let her not leave the church until I have had time to shake hands with everyone else here."

When the service was over, I began to make the rounds, shaking hands with everyone who had come. Sure enough, when I had finished shaking the hands of everyone else, she was still there. When I shook her hand, I placed in it the money God had told me to give her. "The Lord told me to do this," I said.

The sister nearly cried. She said, "I didn't have enough gas to come to church and go home again, but I wanted to come so badly that I told the Lord that I was coming by faith, believing that He would make a way somehow for me to get enough gas to go back home."

I said, "Well, I'm glad I obeyed God, and I know I will be blessed."

That night, when we got to church, our

pastor said that he was going to have a drawing for a five-dollar prize and gave us all tickets. I wasn't even thinking about having given the money, yet when the winning ticket was drawn out it was mine. I said, "Praise God! I knew He was going to make a way for me to get my bill money back before I had to have it." He just wanted to see if I was willing to obey and trust Him. If we are concerned about the needs of others and pray for them, God will take care of our needs.

Thank You, Jesus, for the miracle of Your making a way. ❄

- 20 -

THE MIRACLE OF
LITTLE BEING MUCH

*O fear the LORD, ye his saints: for there
is no want to them that fear him.*

Psalms 34:9

One day while I was working at the
factory, the Lord spoke to me to give fifty
cents to a humble 'bobbin hauler.' I was hesitant to give so little, but when I looked in my
purse to get a dollar instead, I found that I
only had about seventy-five cents with me.

It wasn't that I desperately needed the fifty
cents. I had brought some soft drinks with

me for break time. It just seemed so stingy to give someone fifty cents. I had given him a dollar on several occasions when I knew that he needed it. "Let him ask me to borrow the fifty cents," I prayed, "and then I'll give it to him."

When he didn't come by, I prayed, "Lord, let him just come over my way, and then I'll know this is really of You." But he didn't come.

Later, I realized that it was wrong to question God, that He wanted me to listen to His voice and obey Him. What did it matter if the amount was small or great? What was important was my obedience. I failed the test this time around.

After work that day my sister rode home with me, and as we were walking out to the car, she said, "You'll never guess what happened to me today. The Lord spoke to me to give one of the men fifty cents before the first break. I was very hesitant to give such a little amount, but finally I did it. I'm so glad I did because he was very grateful. He had been very hot and thirsty, but he didn't have money to buy a drink."

I really felt badly in that moment, and I told my sister what had happened. I had disobeyed because I thought that fifty cents was too little to give. I asked God to forgive me and help me to obey Him no matter how large or how small the required sacrifice. He knows what we can do. Little is much, when God is in it. Thank You, Jesus, for the miracle of little being much. ✱

THE MIRACLE OF GIVING WHEN THERE IS A NEED

I have showed you all things, how that so labouring ye ought to support the weak, and to remember the words of the Lord Jesus, how he said, It is more blessed to give than to receive. Acts 20:35

Not long after that at the plant one day the Lord told me to go upstairs and give my sister two dollars. I said, "But, Lord, she probably has more money than I do. Two dollars is all I have left, and my gas tank is nearly empty. I don't even know if I can make it home if I give all my money away."

When the Lord kept dealing with me to give her the money, I again made a bargain with Him. "If You really want me to give her this money, let her come downstairs near my place of work during breaktime. Sometimes she came down, and sometimes she didn't, so I felt that would be a good way of knowing God's will.

Although my sister didn't come down at breaktime, I kept feeling I should go upstairs and take the money to her. I remembered my failure a few days before with the fifty cents, and I didn't want to disobey God again. I had promised Him then that I would be faithful the next time He spoke to me, and now I was hesitating again. I decided to take the plunge.

"Lord," I prayed, "I will trust You to help me have enough gas to get home. I'm going upstairs to give this two dolalrs, even though I don't know why."

I obeyed, going upstairs and giving the two dollars to my sister. "I don't know why,"

I told her, "but God spoke to me to come upstairs and give you this two dollars."

Tears filled her eyes, as she said, "Thank You, Jesus!"

When I asked her why she was so happy, she told me that she had been walking back and forth on her job asking God to help her have enough gas to go to the revival meeting. He had heard that prayer.

Before I left her that day, another worker came over and, not knowing what I had just done, put some more money in my sister's hand. God had known that my two dollars was not enough and had moved on someone else to give her more. She started shouting and dancing before the Lord right there on the job.

We were all happy that day. Truly *it is more blessed to give than receive.* Thank You, Jesus, for the miracle of giving when there is a need.

- 22 -

THE MIRACLE OF GOD'S PROVISION FOR A CHILD

And it shall come to pass, that before they call, I will answer; and while they are yet speaking, I will hear. Isaiah 65:24

When my grandson, Joshua, was in the fifth grade at Brogden Middle School, his class went on a field trip to Chapel Hill, North Carolina.

When his parents went to pick him up that evening, they noticed that he was very excited. The children had all enjoyed the trip, but Joshua had something else on his mind. He had in his hands a very elaborate puzzle about space.

"Where did you get that?" his mother asked, knowing that he hadn't taken any spending money along.

"My friend's dad got it for me," he answered.

As it turned out, they had all gone into a souvenir shop and each of the children had bought something except Joshua.

"Don't you want to buy anything?" the man had asked.

He had gone along on the trip as a chaperone. When he learned that Joshua had no money, he told him to pick out something he would like to have, and he would pay for it.

Joshua knew that Jesus had blessed him and told his parents so. Thank You, Jesus, for Your provision for a child.   ❋

23

THE MIRACLE OF RESTORATION

Ye are of God, little children, and have overcome them: because greater is he that is in you, than he that is in the world.

1 John 4:4

One year John planted some tomato plants in the garden, and they were doing very well—until we got a hard frost one night. Then, most of the plants died. If we had known the frost was coming, he could have covered the plants, but we had no advance warning.

John was concerned about how to buy

more tomato plants, but I assured him that God would help us. We would make it a matter of prayer.

When we went to church that night, we didn't tell anyone about the frost killing our tomato plants, but after the service as we were greeting the others who were there that night, someone put a bill in John's hand. When he got in the van he looked at it and found that it was $20.

"I wonder what they gave me this for?" he said.

"Praise God," I answered, "We were praying for God to help you get some more tomato plants. God saw your heart and knows you love and serve Him. The devil meant to do you harm, but God made a blessing out of it and gave you more than enough to get the plants back."

John bought his plants and had money left over. When we become children of God and have Him living inside of us, we have the promise: *Greater is He that is in you than he that is in the world.* Our God is so good, and we have nothing to fear.

Thank You, Jesus, for the miracle of restoration.   ✸

24

THE MIRACLE OF THE LOST KEY

And whatsoever ye shall ask in my name,
that will I do, that the Father may be glo-
rified in the Son.   John 14:13

When we decided to give up a safety deposit box at the bank, the record showed that we had received two keys when we rented the box. That had been six years before, and we didn't remember getting a second key and had no idea where it might be now. If we couldn't find it and return it, we were told, it would cost us $20. I didn't have the $20, so I told the clerk we would find and return the key.

"I can give you until tomorrow," she said. "If you can't find the other key by then, you'll have to pay the fee."And if you don't come back tomorrow with either the key or the payment, there is a fee of $150."

I started praying: "Oh, Jesus, You have got to help me find that key."

We were on our way to the service in the rest home in Smithfield, so we didn't have more time to think about it right then, but the matter kept coming back to my mind throughout the evening.

When we got home that night, it was already late, but I started looking for the key. I searched through all my old purses, but I couldn't find it. After searching quite a while, I went back into the living room, sat down, and said to John, "I will just have to get the money someway and pay. I can't find the key."

But something about giving up like that didn't seem right. God had done too many miracles for me. He is so faithful and has never let us down. As I thought about it some more, I remembered a year or two before finding a small envelope in my purse. It had been empty, so I threw it away. Maybe the key had fallen out of the envelope into the bottom of the purse. I hadn't been looking for a loose key, but for a bank envelope. I got up and resumed my search.

Sure enough, before long I found it. It had fallen out into the purse and without the envelope in which it had come, I didn't recognize it for what it was. That night I slept well.

Thank You, Jesus, for the miracle of the lost key.   ❊

THE MIRACLE OF
THE RUNAWAY
LOG TRUCK

For with God nothing shall be impossible.   Luke 1:37

Early one morning in 1997, Jimmy was driving a fully-loaded log truck down an exit ramp in Durham, North Carolina, when a van swerved around him and back into his path. In order not to hit the van, he pulled the truck sharply left, and it tipped over and went out of control.

The straps holding the logs in place on the

trailer broke loose and half of the logs careened across the median strip of Route 15-501, while the other half flew down the exit ramp in every direction.

Pinned beneath the steering wheel of the truck, Jimmy could hear screeching brakes and flying logs all around him. A car traveling in the northbound lane had been unable to see the logs in time and had wrecked, too.

When the first policeman arrived at the scene of the accident and approached the tractor, he fully expected to see the driver beheaded or disemboweled. The tractor was so badly damaged that he didn't think anyone could have survived the accident.

Seeing that Jimmy was alive, the policeman encouraged him not to move until the ambulance arrived. But Jimmy was anxious to get out of there because the engine was smoking, and he was afraid it might catch on fire. He asked the policeman to help him get his legs free. The policeman was hesitant, thinking that Jimmy might have broken bones, but when Jimmy insisted, he helped him work his way free. Aside from a lot of bumps and bruises, my son was unhurt and walked away from the accident.

As the wrecker was towing the tractor away, a car pulled up alongside and shouted to the driver, "I know that no one was alive in that truck."

He shouted back, "Believe it or not, he's right here beside me."

Thank You, Jesus, for the miracle of a runaway log truck. ✤

26

THE MIRACLE OF
A GOOD NIGHT'S SLEEP

*It is vain for you to rise up early, to sit
up late, to eat the bread of sorrows: for so
he giveth his beloved sleep.*

Psalms 127:2

One night when John went to bed, his
arms, hands, legs, and feet were hurting so
much that he couldn't get to sleep. He hadn't
been sleeping well for several nights, so he
asked me to pray with him. After we prayed,
he was still hurting.

I waited a while and then asked him again
if he was still hurting. When he said he was,

I got angry with the devil who was afflicting him. I said, "Devil, you are a liar, and by Jesus' stripes he is healed."

I got up and found some anointing oil and began to anoint his hands and feet, all the while, rebuking the enemy. "Devil, take your hands off of him. He is God's property, and in the name of Jesus I command him to quit hurting and be healed and to get a good night's sleep."

John was praying, too, but within ten minutes he was sound sleep. He slept better that night than he had in many days.

Our God hears and answers prayer.

Thank You, Jesus, for the miracle of a good night's sleep.   ❋

27

THE MIRACLE OF HAVING A SONG IN OUR HEARTS

And he hath put a new song in my mouth, even praise unto our God: many shall see it, and fear, and shall trust in the LORD.

Psalms 40:3

One day I was praying for a family of people who had once been Christians but had turned back to the world. I was asking God to deal with their hearts and bring them back to Him. When I had finished praying, God gave me a song for such people. The song lets those of us who stray from the fold know that God still loves us and is waiting with outstretched arms to receive us back to His heart. If we will just seek Him with our whole hearts, we will find Him right where we left Him. He hasn't gone anywhere.

I pray that those who may be reading these pages and find themselves away from God might consider carefully the words God has given me and might rededicate their lives to Him.

Have You Strayed Away from Jesus?

1. *Have you strayed away from Jesus?*
   Are you no longer in His fold?
   Well, I just want to tell you
   He still loves you, and He wants to save
   your soul.
   You'll find Him where you left Him when
   you seek with all of your heart.
   Just ask Him to forgive you, and make a
   brand new start.

2. *Though Satan rages and there're battles*
   up ahead,

Annie Hill Davis

With your trust in Jesus, you have nothing now to dread.
You might stumble, and you might even fall,
But Jesus will be right there to pick you up
When on Him you call.

Chorus:
Shine your light,
Shine your light,
Shine your light that others might see
The glory of God revealed through thee.
He'll be with you on the mountain and in the valley, too
And as long as you hold on to Jesus
There's nothing you can't go through.

Thank You, Jesus, for having a song in our hearts. ❀

- 28 -

THE MIRACLE OF
A THANKFUL CHILD

*Train up a child in the way he should go:
and when he is old, he will not depart
from it.*   Proverbs 22:6

Brenda Carol, our youngest daughter, accepted Jesus at a very early age. She was
only five when she asked Him to forgive her
and save her. Since then, during the past
twenty-two years, she has loved and served
the Lord. I thank God for her every day of
my life, and for my other children, too.
Brenda especially has been a blessing to her
father and me, having lived with us longer
than any of the others.

Annie Hill Davis

Several weeks ago, we wanted to attend the campmeeting in Ashland, Virginia. She was unable to go, but she wanted to pay for the gasoline so that we could go. Then, while we were away, she wrote a poem for us to express her gratitude:

Mama and Daddy, You Are a Blessing

I love you both more than words could say,
More and more every day.
The things you do and the things you say,
Let me know you love me the same way.

I thank God for the both of you,
And the many prayers you've prayed
For God to watch me and keep me safe.
He blessed me with you both,
And I praise him every day.

You've always taught me right from wrong,
And let me know I'm never alone.
Jesus is with us everyday
To lead us and guide us all along the way.
So every day I thank the Lord for you both.

The Little Book of Miracles

You are the best parents in the whole wide world.
And I'm blessed that you are mine.

> *I love you* ♥
> *Your daughter,*
> *Brenda Carol*

As a mother, this made me very proud. I thank God for giving me the wisdom to raise Brenda in a way that she would be thankful to us and to God. I wish more children would thank God for their parents who try to raise them right and that more parents would be thankful to God for their children who are a blessing from Him.

I am grateful to God for my own parents and have always felt the great responsibility to train my own children in the right way and to teach them right from wrong. We have the promise that *when they are old, they will not depart from it*. When we love Jesus, we can love our children enough to motivate us to bring them up right, and then to trust that they will do the right thing.

Thank You, Jesus, for the miracle of a thankful child. ❁

- 29 -

THE MIRACLE OF
A STORY RETOLD

*Then Peter opened his mouth, and said,
Of a truth I perceive that God is no respecter of persons: But in every nation he
that feareth him, and worketh righteous-
ness, is accepted with him.*

Acts 10:34-35

One Monday morning I took my son,
Bobby, to the emergency room in Goldsboro,
North Carolina, to get his hand X-rayed and
see if it had been seriously injured in an accident the day before. If it had not been for the
mercy of God, both he and his nephew, Jodie,

would have been killed in the accident. I hadn't planned to go inside the hospital with him. I thought that I would just sit outside in the van and wait, but he insisted, so I went in. I was glad I did when a lady in the waiting room (named Eleanor Lewis) began to ask me questions.

"I know that you're a Christian," she began.

"Yes, I am," I answered.

She told me about her parents who were Christians, and I told her about my son's accident and how God had spared his life.

She was very eager to hear about the miracles of God, so I went on to tell her of other miracles that God had done for me through the years. There were countless miracles that I could not remember, but those that I could, I told.

The two of us had a good time talking together that day. She enjoyed hearing the stories, and I was blessed in the retelling of them.

I told her about wanting to go to Israel, about putting it on my prayer list, without knowing how it would be financially possible to go, and about how God made a way for

Annie Hill Davis

me, sent me on the trip, and then helped me
to pay all the expenses involved. I told her of
God's protection for my children and His
provision for us in times of need.

That day I began to realize that I needed
to tell the stories of God's goodness to others, that I needed to show Him my gratitude
by telling what He had done.

I could never tell everything, for that
would take forever. God has been my everything, my all. How can you write that down
on paper?

The thing I felt strongly was that if God
would show His favor to me, He would do it
for another as well. He is *no respecter of persons.* What He does for one, He will do for
all.

If we cannot each somehow be a blessing
to those around, what meaning does our life
here have? Surely we are each called to share
God's favor, not only to be blessed here, but
to be a blessing to others as well.

For many years, I have asked God to help
me live a life that would be pleasing to Him
and that my light would shine so that other
people would see His love in me. I may not

be one of the great preachers or prophets of this world, but my life comes into daily contact with many others who need God's love, so I can sometimes do what the great preachers and prophets cannot. My one desire is to lift up the name of Jesus, to glorify Him, so that others may know of His goodness.

I trust that the retelling of these simple stories brings Him glory and that many will come to realize how very good God is. May we know that He does answer prayer, that although bad things do sometimes happen to good people, God always has a purpose in it and will be glorified in the end, as we remain faithful to Him and trust His goodness.

I thank God for that day that I met Eleanor. When Bobby finally came out, he said that his hand was just bruised and would be fine. Eleanor and I became close friends and have maintained contact ever since that day. She was a real encouragement in the writing of this story, and I thank God for her.

Thank You, Jesus, for the miracle of a story retold.   ✷

THE MIRACLE OF SALVATION

Let us therefore come boldly unto the throne of grace, that we may obtain mercy, and find grace to help in time of need.   Hebrews 4:16

In closing this volume, I must take time to address those who may not know my Lord. For many poor people, it is sometimes easy to give in to the problems of life. Suffering and loss have a way of draining the strength from us and leaving us feeling very empty and vulnerable. Thank God for Jesus who came to die for us and who, when we decide to trust and serve Him, gives us perfect peace in the midst of life's storms. The prophet Job was devastated by the tragedies that befell him, yet he declared:

> *Though he [God] slay me, yet will I trust in him: but I will maintain mine own ways before him.*   Job 13:15

Self-pity is a very destructive force that only fills us with depression and despair. As Christians, we have the hope of finding solace and help at the *throne of grace*. Nothing could be more important in life.

Without the Lord we are nothing, and life is meaningless. With Him, we can face whatever life hurls at us and remain victorious. And we have the hope of life everlasting.

Don't turn Jesus away today as He knocks on the door of your heart. Open wide to Him, and come to know His greatest miracle, the miracle of salvation.

Thank You, Jesus, for that miracle of miracles, eternal salvation through Your grace.

Amen!